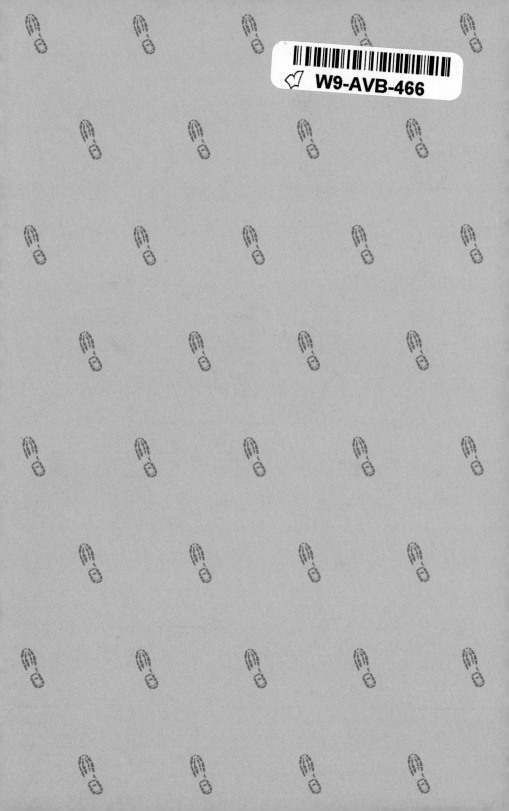

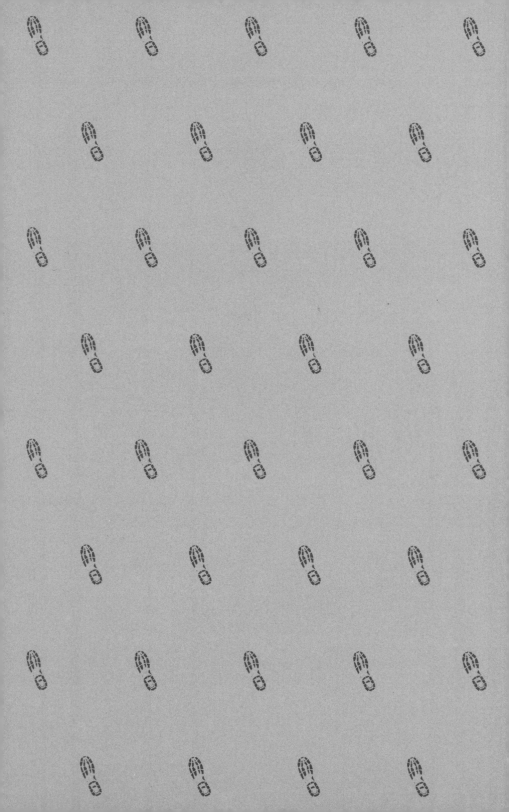

THE NATURE COMPANY
Naturalist's Journal

THE WALKER'S
COMPANION

On the trail marked with pollen, may I walk.
With grasshoppers about my feet, may I walk.
With dew about my feet, may I walk.
With beauty, may I walk.

Navajo Chant

*Three little hills stood near each other, and
down in the midst of them sunk a hollow
basin, almost mathematically circular,
two or three hundred feet in breadth,
and of such depth that a stately
cedar might but just be
visible above the sides.*

The Hollow of the Three Hills,
NATHANIEL HAWTHORNE (1804–64),
American novelist and short-story writer

High up in a sycamore or oak tree, the boisterous and affable acorn woodpecker may be found drilling holes to store winter's rations. It has the ingenious habit of fitting acorns tightly into individual holes, to stop squirrels from prising them out. These larder acorns comprise the main winter diet, when insect populations are low. Woodpeckers live in colonies of three to ten birds where all the work, as well as the rewards, are shared. The acorn woodpecker is found in the open oak and pine-oak forests throughout California and parts of Arizona, New Mexico, and western Texas.

Nature is to be found in her entirety
nowhere more than in her
smallest creatures.

PLINY THE ELDER (AD 23–79),
Roman naturalist and writer

What would the world be, once bereft
Of wet and wilderness? Let them be left,
O let them be left, wilderness and wet;
Long live the weeds and the wilderness yet.

Inversnaid,
GERARD MANLEY HOPKINS (1844–89),
English poet

The great blue heron can be found throughout North America, except in the northern tundra and the most arid stretches of desert. It lives in wetlands among tall reeds and trees that provide protection for the heronry. Great blue herons often nest in company with other species of heron, returning each year to the same cluster of trees. They feed on fish, frogs, reptiles, small mammals, and occasionally other birds.

When visiting an area where herons nest, don't be surprised to find frog bones, or other tidbits from a young heron's meal, come tumbling down from the treetops.

The walking of which I speak has nothing
in it akin to taking exercise, as it is called,
as the sick take medicine at stated
hours... but is itself the enterprise
and adventure of the day.

Walking,
HENRY DAVID THOREAU (1817–62),
American writer and naturalist

One way to open your eyes is to ask yourself, "What if I had never seen this before? What if I knew I would never see it again?"

RACHEL CARSON (1907–64),
American biologist and writer

...the rare moment is not the moment when there is something worth looking at but the moment when we are capable of seeing it.

The Desert Year,
JOSEPH WOOD KRUTCH (1893–1970),
American naturalist

Walker's Notes

The black-footed ferret is one of the rarest mammals in North America, mostly due to the dramatic reduction in prairie dogs, the animals on which it preys. Today, the black-footed ferret is most likely to be found in parts of Montana, South Dakota, Wyoming, and Colorado. Fortunately, ferret populations are being increased by captive breeding programs, but their ecosystem still needs to be protected to ensure survival. The ferret has a distinctive black "Lone Ranger" mask across its eyes, similar to that of a raccoon.

...tired at last, he sat on the bank, while the river still chattered on to him, a babbling procession of the best stories in the world, sent from the heart of the earth to be told at last to the insatiable sea.

The Wind in the Willows,
KENNETH GRAHAME (1859–1932),
English novelist

The killdeer's nest is a scrape on the ground, made up of a jumble of pebbles, some grass, and twigs. There are usually three to five buff, spotted eggs in the nest which are incubated by both parents until they hatch at 24–28 days. Killdeer chicks are already conversing in peeps for a couple of days before they hatch, while at the same time learning to recognize the sound of their parents' voices.

If you approach newly hatched killdeer chicks too closely, the parents may perform a "distraction" display, designed to divert predators and protect the young.

It was the cool gray dawn, and there was a delicious sense of repose and peace in the deep pervading calm and silence of the woods. Not a leaf stirred; not a sound obtruded upon great Nature's meditation.

Tom Sawyer,
MARK TWAIN (1835–1910),
American writer and humorist

The flowers of California buckeye attract a variety of colorful bird and insect life, including the Chalcedon checkerspot butterfly. The striking orange, yellow, and black wings of the checkerspot make a wonderful contrast to the apple-green leaves of buckeye. Checkerspots are found in desert hills, open oak and pine woodlands, and alpine tundra, on figwort, plantain, and honeysuckle host plants as well as buckeye.

Although not harmful to the insects and birds that feed on them, the seeds of the California buckeye are highly toxic to humans.

From this day forth
I shall be called a wanderer,
Leaving on a journey
Thus among the early showers.

<small>BASHO (1644–94),
Japanese poet and diarist</small>

We need the tonic of wilderness, to wade
sometimes in marshes where the bittern
and the meadow-hen lurk, and hear
the booming of the snipe...

Walden,
HENRY DAVID THOREAU (1817–62),
American writer and naturalist

With lively feelings, may I walk.
As it used to be long ago, may I walk.
Happily may I walk.

NAVAJO CHANT

River otters work and play hard,
even though it may seem that they
are constantly having fun. They
communicate with mates or siblings
by soft chuckles, apparently as a
sign of affection, along with growls,
grunts, and snorts in an effort to
make their point. A river otter's diet
consists primarily of fish, along
with crayfish, salamanders, and frogs
found while poking along the river
bottom. Otters tend to eat larger
catches on land, while smaller meals
are consumed in the river. They can
also be seen running around on dry
land, and have been known to raid
the nests of birds, turtles, and rabbits.

...*dreamily he fell to considering what a nice snug
dwelling-place it would make for an animal
with few wants and fond of a bijou
riverside residence, above flood level
and remote from noise and dust.*

The Wind in the Willows,
KENNETH GRAHAME (1859–1932),
English novelist

Land, then, is not merely soil; it is a fountain of energy flowing through a circuit of soils, plants, and animals.

ALDO LEOPOLD (1888–1948),
American conservationist and writer

Walker's Notes

Among the most fascinating bog
inhabitants are insectivorous plants,
which supplement their diet drawn
from the nutrient-poor soils by
digesting insects.

One such plant, the pitcher plant,
ranges throughout the eastern US
and southern Canada, from
Saskatchewan to Labrador. Its large
leaves form a vertical tube. Insects
are lured into the tube by its
brightly colored entrance and by
the nectar. Once inside, they are
trapped by the downward-pointing
hairs lining the slippery walls, and
often drown in water at the bottom.
They then gradually decompose and
are absorbed by the plant's leaves.

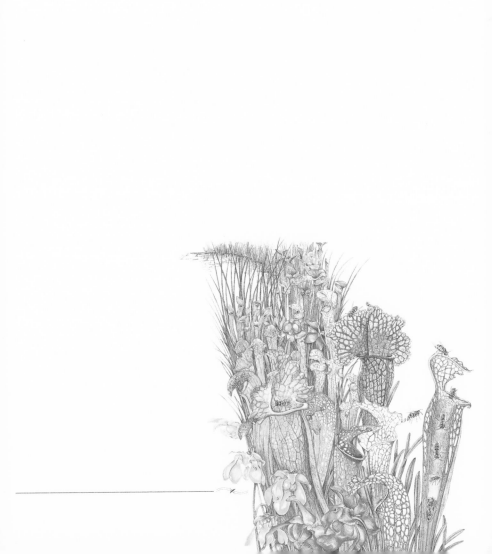

Nature is always hinting at us. It hints over and over again. And suddenly we take the hint.

ROBERT FROST (1874–1963),
American poet

The moon was bright, the air was free,
And fruits and flowers together grew
On many a shrub and many a tree:
And all put on a gentle hue,
Hanging in the shadowy air
Like a picture rich and rare.

Encinctured with a Twine of Leaves,
SAMUEL TAYLOR COLERIDGE (1772–1834),
English poet

Painted turtles love to bask on half-submerged logs in the sun, often in line formation or piled on top of each other, so these strikingly colored creatures are easily spotted in the wild. They are found in the shallow, quiet waters of ponds, rivers, lakes, and streams from the far south of the US to the southern parts of Canada. They are the most abundant of all the turtles in North America. Their food consists mainly of aquatic vegetation, snails, insects, and crayfish. Young turtles are primarily carnivorous, becoming herbivores as they mature.

Enjoy thy stream, O harmless fish;
And when an angler for his dish,
  Through gluttony's vile sin,
Attempts, a wretch, to pull thee out,
God give thee strength, O gentle trout,
  To pull the rascal in!

JOHN WALCOTT (1738–1819),
English writer

Walker's Notes

The desert pupfish inhabits the
marshy backwaters of desert springs
and streams in California, Arizona,
and Mexico. It is thought to have
survived from the last ice age when
the streams were fresh and much
larger than they are today. This fish
has adapted for survival in high
salinity and the temperatures of
today's desert streams. The desert
pupfish grows quickly, reaching up
to 2 inches (5 cm) in a year, which
is almost its full length—up to
2½ inches (6.5 cm).

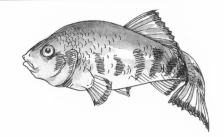

Afoot and light-hearted I take to the open road,
Healthy, free, the world before me,
The long brown path before me leading
  Wherever I choose.

"Song of the Open Road" from *Leaves of Grass,*
WALT WHITMAN (1819–92),
American poet, journalist, and essayist

American black bears are excellent
tree climbers. Mother bears often
send their cubs to safety up a tree
when danger threatens. The cubs
remain there, waiting for their
mother, who has made her own
escape, returning when it is safe.
Black bears also like to snooze in
trees, as it is difficult for someone to
surprise them up there. In the East,
black bears tend to be almost black,
while in the West, they vary from
black to cinnamon. Although classed
as carnivores, black bears mostly feed
on buds, leaves, nuts, and roots.

All the wisdom of the dead civilizations is nothing to what the robin's song tells, if you will but listen.

The Lone Swallows,
HENRY WILLIAMSON (1897–1977),
English novelist and nature writer

The plants and animals that live in high mountain areas and arctic environments face severe cold, wind, and snow for nine months of the year, with summer appearing as but the briefest of interludes.

Birds such as the Bohemian waxwing cope by descending to the valley floors, where conditions are milder than in the highlands and there is greater access to food and nesting areas. The waxwing feeds on insects and berries found in the coniferous forests of Canada and the Rockies. It is known to occasionally roam, within the flock, far to the south and east of its usual range.

The influence of fine scenery, the presence
of mountains, appeases our irritations
and elevates our friendships.

"Culture" from *The Conduct of Life*,
RALPH WALDO EMERSON (1803–82),
American poet, essayist, and philosopher

The field has eyes, the wood has ears;
I will look, be silent, and listen.

HIERONYMUS BOSCH (1450–1516),
Flemish artist

The brackish-water fiddler crab strongly prefers brackish-water mud habitats, unlike other fiddlers that more commonly prefer sandy beaches and estuaries. The brackish-water fiddler is about 1½ inches (4 cm) wide, and 1 inch (2.5 cm) long, and its carapace is almost rectangular. One of the male's two pincers is distinctively larger than the other, and is white, with uneven projections on the inner surface. Both the female's pincers are of the same size and color. The brackish-water fiddler crab is a tannish-brown above and gray at the front, with olive-colored walking legs.

The uptorn trees are not rooted again;
the parted hills are left scarred; if
there is a new growth, the trees
are not the same as the old,
and the hills underneath their
green vesture bear the
marks of the past rending.

Mill on the Floss,
GEORGE ELIOT (1819–80),
English novelist

Oxen that rattle the yoke and chain or
* halt in the leafy shade, what is*
that you express in your eyes
It seems to me more than all the print I
* have read in my life.*

"Song of Myself" from *Leaves of Grass,*
WALT WHITMAN (1819–92),
American poet, journalist, and essayist

One of the most beautiful birds in Hawaii is the iiwi, with its brilliant red feathers and long, downward-curving beak that can easily reach the nectar in trumpet-shaped flowers. The iiwi's song sounds a bit like a rusty windmill creaking in the breeze. Another Hawaiian bird, the amakihi, has a mellow song that moves up and down the musical scale, while the diminutive elepaio's tune is more like a sharp whistle.

The kipuka—luxuriant forest that is home to these three birds—lies on the slopes of the volcanoes Mauna Loa and Mauna Kea, providing a fertile, shaded environment.

...unless the soul goes out to meet what we see we do not see it; nothing do we see, not a beetle, not a blade of grass.

The Book of a Naturalist,
WILLIAM HENRY HUDSON (1841–1922),
English writer

Walker's Notes

The zebratail lizard is a large lizard,
6–9 inches (15–23 cm) in length.
It lives in the desert areas of central
Nevada and southwest Utah, south
to Arizona and southeast from
California into Mexico.

Zebratails are good runners, and
when they take off, they do so at
very high speeds on their hind legs.
This lizard will curl up its tail and
wag it when startled, showing its
black stripes, as evidence of its
distress. Zebratails eat smaller
lizards, insects, spiders, and flowers.

*Not only the days, but life itself lengthens
in summer. I would spread abroad my
arms and gather more of it
to me, could I do so.*

The Life of the Fields,
RICHARD JEFFERIES (1848–87),
English naturalist and novelist

Winter is no mere negation, no mere absence of summer;
it is another and a positive presence.

The Outermost House,
HENRY BESTON (1888–1968),
American writer

Ten thousand flowers in spring,
the moon in autumn,
a cool breeze in summer,
snow in winter.
If your mind isn't clouded
by unnecessary things,
this is the best season
of your life.

WU-MEN (1183–1260),
Chinese poet

Walker's Notes

⤬

Western tanagers belong to a very
colorful group of birds of which
the females are often almost as
spectacular as the males. While a few
related US species are migratory,
most are not. However, along with
the closely related summer and
scarlet tanagers, the western tanager
makes annual visits to Mexico and
Central America. It nests in the
deciduous and open coniferous
forests of western North America,
feeding on insects in the warmer
months and berries and fruit during
winter when insects may be scarce.

The forest, as usual, had little to intercept the
view below the branches, but the tall straight
trunks of trees. Everything belonging to
vegetation had struggled toward
the light, and beneath the leafy
canopy one walked, as it might be,
through a vast natural vault,
that was upheld by myriads
of rustic columns.

JAMES FENIMORE COOPER (1789–1851),
American novelist

See thou bring not to field or stone
The fancies found in books;
Leave authors' eyes, and fetch your own,
To brave the landscape's looks.

Waldeinsamkeit,
RALPH WALDO EMERSON (1803–82),
American poet, essayist, and philosopher

Perhaps the most familiar goose to most North Americans, the Canada goose is remarkable for its great variations in size. Some of the largest subspecies are nearly twice as big as the smallest—the small subspecies are 22–26 inches (56–66 cm) long, while larger subspecies may reach up to 35–45 inches (90–115 cm) in length. All Canada geese have the diagnostic white "chinstrap" and are varying shades of brown below. If you spot a flock of "wild geese" migrating to their wintering range, you will usually find them to be Canada geese.

The opportunity to see geese is more important than television, and the chance to find a pasque-flower is a right as inalienable as free speech.

A Sand County Almanac,
ALDO LEOPOLD (1886–1948),
American conservationist and writer

A woodland in full color is awesome as a forest fire, in magnitude at least; but a single tree is like a dancing tongue of flame to warm the heart.

"Autumn in Your Hand" from *Sundial of the Seasons,*
HAL BORLAND (1900–78),
American naturalist

Named for the male's red "start," which is the old English word for tail, the redstart is, in summer, one of North America's most common warblers. Redstarts favor deciduous and mixed second-growth woodlands where they set up territories after returning from wintering in Mexico, Central America, or the Caribbean. The male redstart is quite unusual in that it has the same plumage in summer and winter.

*The night is the winter, the morning
and evening are the spring and fall,
and the noon is the summer.*

Walden,
HENRY DAVID THOREAU (1817–62),
American writer and naturalist

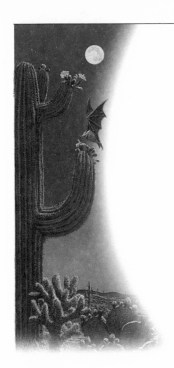

Any fine morning a power saw
can fell a tree that took a
thousand years to grow.

Autumn Across America,
EDWIN WAY TEALE (1899–1980),
American writer and naturalist

Ducks' tails, drakes' tails,
Yellow feet a-quiver,
Yellow bills all out of sight
Busy in the river!

The Wind in the Willows,
KENNETH GRAHAME (1859–1932),
English novelist

The eastern chipmunk is easily
recognized by its reddish-brown fur,
and the dark and light stripes down
the middle of its back. Essentially a
forest dweller, it can sometimes be
seen scooting into cracks in stone
walls and around houses. Although
the eastern chipmunk is a ground
species, it will readily scale oak trees
when the acorns are ripe and
bring them down, bulging from its
cheek pouches, for winter storage.
Eastern chipmunks are also fond
of sweet, juicy blueberries.

How many hearts with warm red blood
in them are beating under cover
of the woods, and how many
teeth and eyes are shining!

The Yosemite,
JOHN MUIR (1838–1914),
Scottish-born American naturalist and writer

Walker's Notes

In summertime, look for eastern bluebirds in open woods, especially where there are pines, east of the Rocky Mountains from southern Canada to the Gulf of Mexico.

Plumage is a striking, bright blue above with a reddish-brown breast and white belly. The song of the eastern bluebird is a gentle, melodic warble, while its distinctive call is a tuneful *turee* or *queedle*. The bird's presence in early spring is a longed-for sign of winter's end.

*...I dressed and went for a walk—determined
not to return until I took what
Nature had to offer.*

This Morning,
RAYMOND CARVER (1938–88),
American writer and poet

Your nature rambles will be more rewarding if the proper equipment is used. Sensible, waterproof walking shoes and socks make a great contribution to your comfort and well-being. Binoculars are also a must, no matter where you go, but are particularly valuable on saltwater marshes and estuaries, because coastal wetlands support a staggering variety of bird life that is hard to get close to. Properly cared for, a good quality pair of binoculars should last a lifetime.

*I believe a leaf of grass is no less than
the journey-work of the stars...*

"Song of Myself" from *Leaves of Grass,*
WALT WHITMAN (1819–92),
American poet

...The bee,
A more adventurous colonist than man,
With whom he came across the eastern deep,
Fills the savannas with his murmurings,
And hides his sweets, as in the golden age,
Within the hollow oak.

The Prairies,
WILLIAM CULLEN BRYANT (1754–1812),
American poet, critic, and editor

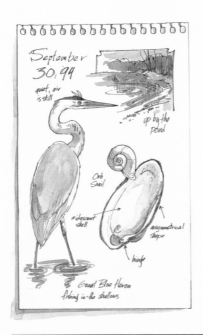

September
30, 94

quiet, air
is still

up by the
pond

Orb
Snail

iridescent
shell

asymmetrical
shape

hinge

Great Blue Heron
fishing in the shallows

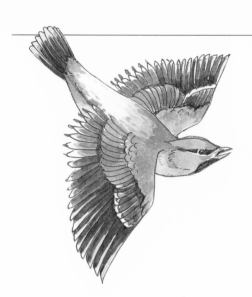

ᵤ lucky enough to sight many ᵢ your walks (remember, most are ᵤ and come out to feed at dawn ᵤusk), but there's a definite possibility you'll ᵢe their tracks. Early morning provides the best tracking conditions. The ground is still damp then, especially after rain or a snowfall has provided a clean surface for new tracks. Investigate the places that meet mammals' needs for food, shelter, and water, and examine soft ground where an impression might have been made.

Red Fox

Foreprint about 2¼ inches (5.5 cm) long, hindprint slightly smaller. Members of the dog family can't retract their claws, so the four-toed prints of domestic dogs, coyotes, foxes, and wolves all feature claw marks. In heavy snow, the animal's tail may brush out tracks.

Deer
Foreprint 2–3 inches (5–7.5 cm) long, hindprint is slightly smaller. Hoofed animals leave two-toed tracks; white-tailed deer, moose, and caribou also leave dewclaw imprints that are made by vestigial toes behind the main toes.

Virginia Opossum
Hindprint no more than 2 inches (5 cm) wide, foreprint slightly smaller. Opossums and raccoons leave five-toed tracks and walk flat-footed, as do most members of the weasel family.

Grizzly Bear
Hindprint of a large grizzly may be 11 inches (27.5 cm) long and 8 inches (20 cm) wide. In soft mud, the bear makes an even larger impression. Bears walk flat-footed.

Porcupine
Foreprint, including claw marks, about 2½ inches (6.5 cm) long, hindprint at least 3 inches (7.5 cm) long. Porcupines may drag their feet in snow, and their belly and tail may also blur their trail.

Florida Panther
3 inches wide by 3 inches long (7.5 × 7.5 cm). Cats leave a four-toed pad impression, without claws.

Prairie Dog
Hindprint 1¼ inches (3 cm) long with five toes, foreprint slightly smaller, with four toes. A tail-drag mark may also be seen.

Bighorn sheep
Foreprints 3–3½ inches (7.5–9 cm) long, hindprints slightly smaller. Dewclaws may print two dots on soft ground.

Gray Wolf
Foreprint 4¼–5 inches (10.5–12.5 cm) long, hindprint slightly smaller.

Black-footed Ferret
Hindprint is 2 inches (5 cm) long and about 1½ inches (4cm) wide. Foreprint is about the same length, but narrower. The five-toed prints show claw marks.

Caribou
Crescent-shaped prints 5 inches (12.5 cm) long. Usually followed by dewclaw marks. Caribou may leave a double impression about 8 inches (20 cm) long because their hindprints often overlap their foreprints.

Beaver
The webbed hind feet leave a fan shape more than 5 inches (13 cm) wide, and twice as long as the foreprints. The drag mark of the tail may also be seen.

Kangaroo Rat
Hindprint about 1½ inches (4 cm) long, foreprints much smaller. Foreprint may not print if the animal is hopping. The tail may leave a drag mark.

The Nature Company Naturalist's Journals are published by Time-Life Books

Conceived and produced by Weldon Owen Pty Limited
43 Victoria Street, McMahons Point, NSW, 2060, Australia
A member of the Weldon Owen Group of Companies
Sydney • San Francisco
Copyright 1997 © US Weldon Owen Inc.
Copyright 1997 © Weldon Owen Pty Ltd

THE NATURE COMPANY
Priscilla Wrubel, Ed Strobin, Steve Manning,
Georganne Papac, Tracy Fortini, Deanna Pervis

TIME-LIFE BOOKS
Time-Life Books is a division of Time Life Inc.
Time-Life is a trademark of Time Warner Inc. U.S.A.

Time-Life Custom Publishing
Vice-President and Publisher: Terry Newell
Director of New Product Development: Regina Hall
Managing Editor: Donia Ann Steele
Director of Sales: Neil Levin
Director of Financial Operations: J. Brian Birky

WELDON OWEN PTY LTD
Publisher: Sheena Coupe
Managing Editor: Lynn Humphries
Project Editor: Liz Connolly
Designers: Clive Collins, Clare Forte

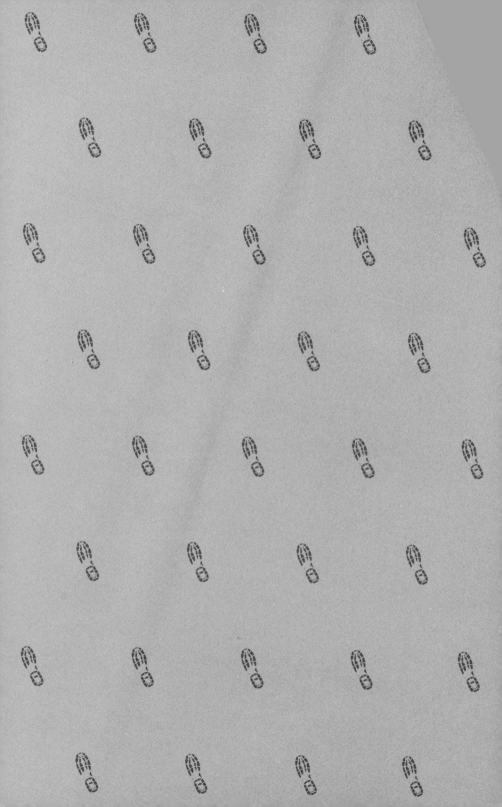

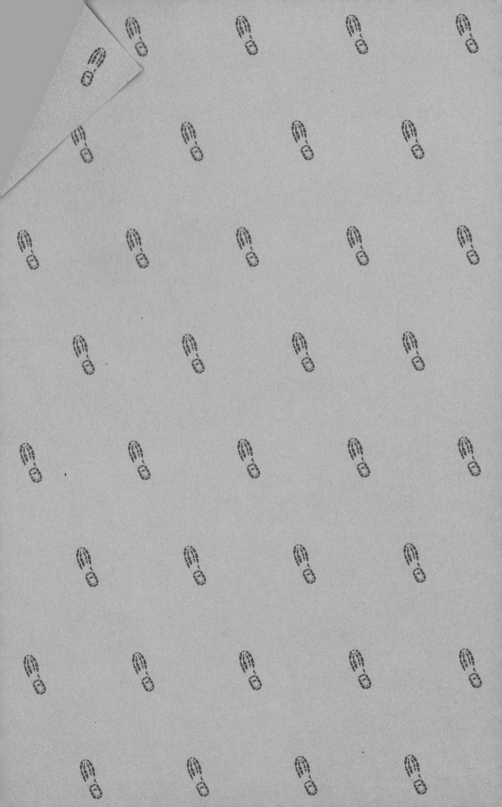